Instrumental Solos for VIOLIN

RODGERS AND HAMMERSTEIN™

THE SOUND OF MUSIC®

How To Use The CD Accompaniment:
A melody cue appears on the right channel only. If your CD player has a balance adjustment,
you can adjust the volume of the melody by turning down the right channel.

ISBN 0-634-02730-1

WILLIAMSON MUSIC®
A RODGERS AND HAMMERSTEIN COMPANY
www.williamsonmusic.com

EXCLUSIVELY DISTRIBUTED BY

HAL•LEONARD® CORPORATION
7777 W. BLUEMOUND RD. P.O. BOX 13819 MILWAUKEE, WI 53213

Visit Hal Leonard Online at
www.halleonard.com

The offering of this publication for sale is not to be construed as authorization for the performance of any material contained herein.
Applications for the right to perform THE SOUND OF MUSIC, in whole or in part, could be addressed to
The Rodgers & Hammerstein Theatre Library
229 West 28th Street, 11th Floor
New York, NY 10001
Tel: 800/400.8160 or 212/564.400 • Fax: 212/268.1245.
E-mail: theatre@rnh.com • Website: www.rnh.com

RODGERS AND HAMMERSTEIN™

THE SOUND OF MUSIC®

Contents

◆ DO-RE-MI

VIOLIN

Lyrics by OSCAR HAMMERSTEIN II
Music by RICHARD RODGERS

❷ THE SOUND OF MUSIC

VIOLIN

Lyrics by OSCAR HAMMERSTEIN II
Music by RICHARD RODGERS

❸ MARIA

VIOLIN

Lyrics by OSCAR HAMMERSTEIN II
Music by RICHARD RODGERS

◆ MY FAVORITE THINGS

VIOLIN

Lyrics by OSCAR HAMMERSTEIN II
Music by RICHARD RODGERS

◆ EDELWEISS

VIOLIN

Lyrics by OSCAR HAMMERSTEIN II
Music by RICHARD RODGERS

With gentle motion

◆ THE LONELY GOATHERD

VIOLIN

Lyrics by OSCAR HAMMERSTEIN II
Music by RICHARD RODGERS

◆⑦ SIXTEEN GOING ON SEVENTEEN

VIOLIN

Lyrics by OSCAR HAMMERSTEIN II
Music by RICHARD RODGERS

◆8 SO LONG, FAREWELL

VIOLIN

Lyrics by OSCAR HAMMERSTEIN II
Music by RICHARD RODGERS

◆9 CLIMB EV'RY MOUNTAIN

VIOLIN

Lyrics by OSCAR HAMMERSTEIN II
Music by RICHARD RODGERS

PLAY ALONG CD COLLECTIONS

BAND JAM

12 band favorites complete with accompaniment CD, including: Born to Be Wild • Danger Zone • Devil with the Blue Dress • Final Countdown • Get Ready for This • Gonna Make You Sweat (Everybody Dance Now) • I Got You (I Feel Good) • Rock & Roll - Part II (The Hey Song) • Twist and Shout • We Will Rock You • Wild Thing • Y.M.C.A.

_____00841232 Flute $10.95
_____00841233 Clarinet $10.95
_____00841234 Alto Sax $10.95
_____00841235 Trumpet $10.95
_____00841236 Horn $10.95
_____00841237 Trombone $10.95
_____00841238 Violin $10.95

DISNEY SOLOS – INTERMEDIATE LEVEL

An exciting collection of 12 solos with professional orchestral accompaniment on CD. Titles include: Be Our Guest • Can You Feel the Love Tonight • Colors of the Wind • Friend like Me • Under the Sea • You've Got a Friend in Me • Zero to Hero • and more.

_____00841404 Flute $12.95
_____00841506 Oboe $12.95
_____00841405 Clarinet/Tenor Sax $12.95
_____00841406 Alto Sax $12.95
_____00841407 Horn $12.95
_____00841408 Trombone $12.95
_____00841409 Trumpet $12.95
_____00841410 Violin $12.95
_____00841411 Viola $12.95
_____00841412 Cello $12.95
_____00841553 Mallet Percussion $12.95

EASY DISNEY FAVORITES

A fantastic selection of 13 Disney favorites for solo instuments, including: Bibbidi-Bobbidi-Boo • Candle on the Water • Chim Chim Cher-ee • A Dream Is a Wish Your Heart Makes • It's a Small World • Let's Go Fly a Kite • Mickey Mouse March • A Spoonful of Sugar • Supercalifragilisticexpialidocious • Toyland March • Winnie the Pooh • The Work Song • Zip-A-Dee-Doo-Dah. Each book features a play-along CD with complete rhythm section accompaniment.

_____00841371 Flute $10.95
_____00841477 Clarinet $10.95
_____00841478 Alto Sax $10.95
_____00841479 Trumpet $10.95
_____00841480 Trombone $10.95
_____00841372 Violin $10.95
_____00841481 Viola $10.95
_____00841482 Cello/Bass $10.95

FAVORITE MOVIE THEMES

13 themes, including: An American Symphony from _Mr. Holland's Opus_ • Braveheart • Chariots of Fire • Forrest Gump – Main Title • Theme from _Jurassic Park_ • Mission: Impossible Theme • and more.

_____00841166 Flute $10.95
_____00841167 Clarinet $10.95
_____00841169 Alto Sax $10.95
_____00841168 Trumpet/Tenor Sax $10.95
_____00841171 Horn $10.95
_____00841170 Trombone $10.95
_____00841296 Violin $10.95

HYMNS FOR THE MASTER

15 inspirational favorites, including: All Hail the Power of Jesus' Name • Amazing Grace • Crown Him With Many Crowns • Joyful, Joyful We Adore Thee • This Is My Father's World • When I Survey the Wondrous Cross • and more.

_____00841136 Flute $12.95
_____00841137 Clarinet $12.95
_____00841138 Alto Sax $12.95
_____00841139 Trumpet $12.95
_____00841140 Trombone $12.95
_____00841239 Piano Accompaniment (no CD)...........$8.95

JAZZ & BLUES

14 songs for solo instruments, complete with a play-along CD. Includes: Bernie's Tune • Cry Me a River • Fever • Fly Me to the Moon • God Bless' the Child • Harlem Nocturne • Moonglow • A Night in Tunisia • One Note Samba • Opus One • Satin Doll • Slightly Out of Tune (Desafinado) • Take the "A" Train • Yardbird Suite.

00841438 Flute $10.95
00841439 Clarinet $10.95
00841440 Alto Sax $10.95
00841441 Trumpet $10.95
00841442 Tenor Sax $10.95
00841443 Trombone $10.95
00841444 Violin $10.95

MAMBO NO. 5, MARIA MARIA, AND OTHER LATIN HITS

These long-awaited play-along book/CD packs feature 10 super hot Latin hits: Genie in a Bottle • I Need to Know • I Wan'na Be like You (The Monkey Song) • If You Had My Love • Mambo No. 5 (A Little Bit Of...) • Mambo Swing • Maria Maria • Mucho Mambo • Para De Jugar • You Sang to Me.

00841526 Flute $10.95
00841527 Clarinet $10.95
00841528 Alto Sax $10.95
00841529 Tenor Sax $10.95
00841530 Trumpet $10.95
00841531 Horn $10.95
00841532 Trombone $10.95
00841533 Violin $10.95

PLAY THE DUKE

Features 11 classics from Duke Ellington's stellar career: Caravan • Don't Get Around Much Anymore • I Got It Bad and That Ain't Good • I'm Beginning to See the Light • In a Sentimental Mood • It Don't Mean a Thing (If It Ain't Got That Swing) • Mood Indigo • Satin Doll • Solitude • Sophisticated Lady • Take the "A" Train.

00841515 Flute $10.95
00841516 Clarinet $10.95
00841517 Alto Sax $10.95
00841518 Tenor Sax $10.95
00841519 Trumpet $10.95
00841520 Horn $10.95
00841521 Trombone $10.95
00841522 Violin $10.95

ROCK JAMS

12 rockin' favorites to jam along with the accompanying CD. Songs include: Addicted to Love • Another One Bites the Dust • Get Ready • Love Shack • What I Like About You • and more.

_____00841251 Flute $10.95
_____00841252 Clarinet/Tenor Sax $10.95
_____00841253 Alto Sax $10.95
_____00841254 Trumpet $10.95
_____00841257 Horn $10.95
_____00841255 Trombone/Baritone $10.95
_____00841256 Violin $10.95

FROM

HAL•LEONARD®
CORPORATION

FOR MORE INFORMATION, SEE YOUR LOCAL MUSIC DEALER, OR WRITE TO:

7777 W. BLUEMOUND RD. P.O. BOX 13819 MILWAUKEE, WI 53213

http://www.halleonard.com